MW01292122

WORLD WAR 1

A History From Beginning to End

BY

HENRY FREEMAN

Copyright © 2016

Table of Contents

Introduction

The First World War, known at the time as "The Great War", was a four-year conflict that spanned the globe-- involving thirty-two countries in total. It was an unforeseen war that resulted from a series of calamities that broke the delicate arrangement of European powers, and ended with the loss of over eleven million military personnel and seven million civilians.

What had started as a diplomatic feud brought on by the assassination of a monarch erupted into a conflict that engulfed the world and changed the map of Europe - forever.

The war brought about revolution; it ended empires, dissolved monarchies and led to the development of war machines that play a crucial role in the modern conflicts of today.

It was thought at the time that the war wouldn't last more than a few months, and that victory would be won easily and without much cost. However as the months turned into years and the war spread like hell-fire, it scorched Europe and surrounding continents. Entire cities were leveled, genocides were committed and exploited for strategic advantage, and all sides were hit with immense losses.

The war quickly became one of attrition, with mass slaughter the strategy and marginal gains the result. It was a new war being fought with old tactics, an industrialized grinding machine that ended the lives of so many.

Follow now as we explore one of the darkest and deadliest periods in modern history--the First World War.

Chapter One

1914 - Blood Is Spilled

The precarious geography of Europe in 1914 was a considerable, and inevitable, catalyst for agitation. On the outset of war, the continent was split by powerful nations and congealed into opposing alliances that faced each other with strong militaristic and industrial vigor.

Europe was divided into two major alliances: The "Triple Entente", an Anglo-Russian agreement between the Russian Empire, the French Third Republic and the United Kingdom of Great Britain and Ireland, and the "Triple Alliance", which was formed of Germany, Austria-Hungary and the Kingdom of Italy.

Prior to the beginning of the twentieth century, Europe had been in a state of total conflict. A great number of wars had been fought to secure land, expand borders and form new countries.

By 1871, the nation of Germany was in its infancy. It had grown from a confederation of German states into an overbearing empire, having massively expanded its industrial and colonial interests.

In 1879, Germany--with a desire for further European and Baltic expansion--took advantage of the waning Austro-Hungarian Empire and formed a "Dual Alliance" to protect against possible Russian aggression in the Baltic regions.

In 1882, Italy, fearing conflict with France after the latter took colonial territory from her in Tunisia, signed the Triple Alliance agreement with Germany and Austria-Hungary. Italy's allegiance to its previous enemy, Austria-Hungary, was met with some incredulity from the Italian public.

The agreement promised the protection of each nation if they were to be attacked by antagonist empires. The Triple Alliance agreement was renewed in 1887, 1907 and 1912. However, in 1902, Italy made a secret pact with France--promising to remain neutral if Germany provoked France. The flimsy agreement of the Triple Alliance had started to falter.

Germany, with an agenda for supporting Austria-Hungary in acquiring land in the Baltic region, fancied itself as the successor to the Austro-Hungarian Empire as it faced a slow but inevitable collapse.

Italy was restless. It viewed its place in Europe as that of an isolated nation; it too had ambitions of becoming an empire and sought to grab territory in the Baltic regions as well as in the Mediterranean and Africa.

In opposition, The Franco-Russian Alliance, signed in 1894, was an agreement that promised that if either nation were to be attacked by a member of the Triple Alliance, each would aid its ally in defense. The treaty also stipulated that should any member of the Triple Alliance begin mass mobilization of its military, France and Russia would respond in kind.

Great Britain had been in a state of "Splendid Isolation" over affairs in Europe. Its interests lay in attaining more land overseas in order to preserve its empire and Commonwealth. But by 1904, Britain had growing concerns about the power the nations of the Triple Alliance had amassed, and was persuaded by France to agree to a treaty. The agreement resolved their conflict over colonial interests in Africa.

The "Entente Cordiale" put an end to centuries of aggression between the two countries and settled significant differences. Meanwhile, the "Anglo-Russian Entente" was a treaty agreed in 1907 between Great Britain and Russia. It settled British and Russian animosities surrounding control of countries in Persia, Mesopotamia and Asia.

The Triple Entente, agreed in 1907, was a somewhat reluctant and partially neutral treaty between Great Britain, France and Russia. The goal was to form a strong counterforce against potential aggression from the Triple Alliance--and to retaliate if any ally were to be attacked by the nations of the Triple Alliance.

To this day, there's still a debate among historians as to which of a plethora of possible events led to the outbreak of the First World War. The most commonly agreed cause, and perhaps the most seismic event, was the assassination of the Arch Duke of Austria-Hungary.

On June 28th, 1914, Arch Duke Franz Ferdinand and his wife, Duchess Sophie Chotek of Austria, were assassinated whilst on a state visit to Sarajevo, in Austro-Hungarian Bosnia. The assassin was a nineteen-year-old nationalist: Gavrilo Princip.

Princip was a member of the Pan-Slavist ultra-nationalist Serbian group known as "The Black Hand Society".

Princip was with seven other would-be assassins that day who also resented the Austro-Hungarian annexation of Bosnia-Herzegovina, and dreamt of a free and independent Serbia and a greater kingdom uniting all Slavs--which became Yugoslavia.

Though there's no doubt that these men, Princip included, acquired their weapons and training in Belgrade, Serbia, history has ruled out any official involvement by the Serbian government in the assassination of the Arch Duke. Nonetheless, Austria-Hungary declared that Serbia was complicit in the assassination and held it accountable.

On the 5th of July, Kaiser Wilhelm II, the emperor of Germany, signed what became known as Germany's "Blank Cheque". He promised full solidarity with Austria-Hungary, even if they declared war on Serbia. The Kaiser decreed that Germany wouldn't yield in its support of Austro-Hungarian aggression into Serbia, even if it resulted in conflict with Russia.

The Hungarian Prime Minister István Tisza, whose approval, among others, was required in order to launch an attack on Serbia, was highly skeptical of any action that could incur the military might of Russia. Instead, he and other Austro-Hungarian leaders elected to issue Serbia an ultimatum. The intention of some was to demand that the ultimatum be so damaging, so humiliating and punishing that Serbia would have no option but to reject it, thus leading to the war that some Austro-Hungarian politicians intently craved.

The ultimatum was tantamount to the loss of Serbian sovereignty to Austria-Hungary. Serbia rejected the impossible ultimatum on the 25th of July, thirty-seven days after the assassination of Arch Duke Ferdinand. Three days later on July 28th, Austria-Hungary declared war on Serbia, though it took some time before she fully mobilized her forces along the border.

In a final effort to avert all-out war across Europe, Sir Edward Grey, the British foreign secretary, proposed peace talks between all sides. However his plea was rejected by Kaiser Wilhelm. War looked inevitable.

Russia began to mobilize her forces; Germany, aware that war with Russia was unavoidable, prepared to fight a war on two fronts knowing that, with Russian involvement, she'd be met with aggression from France.

On the 1st of August, Germany declared war on Russia, and both sides began to mobilize their forces along their respective borders. France also mobilized to face German forces at the border.

In the days that followed, Italy dismantled the delicate pact of the Triple Alliance when, soon after the outbreak of war, she decided to remain neutral and not follow her allies into armed conflict, citing that the purpose of the Triple Alliance was for defense, not aggression.

Germany insisted that Belgium provide passage of German troops through her borders. The plan exercised by Germany, known as "The Schlieffen Plan", was to flank the French forces mobilized along the border by entering Belgium and circling behind the French front, then after what was planned to be a quick defeat, Germany would withdraw vast swaths of her military to meet the Russians.

The Treaty of London, signed in 1839, was an agreement brokered by Great Britain between the major nations of Europe, guaranteeing Belgium's neutrality and sovereignty after she broke away from the United Kingdom of the Netherlands. The Schlieffen Plan, that had been in development for nine years prior to the war, ignored Belgium's neutrality and was considered an act of war. Britain demanded that Germany cease her march into Belgium and withdraw. On the 4th of August, after Germany ignored the demands to halt the incursion, Britain declared war on Germany.

Germany's first attack was an assault on the town of Liège. The heavily fortified area held off the German offensive by about five days, though it sustained heavy losses for its efforts. Liège fell on the 16th of August, which granted German forces uninterrupted passage to France.

France initiated Plan 17, a long-standing plan of mobilization in the event of war with Germany. French forces crossed the German frontier, unaware that Germany was planning to enter France via Belgium. The head-on assault incurred substantial losses on both sides, and France retreated.

Britain and France declared war on Austria-Hungary on the 12th of August. Following the declaration, a British Expeditionary Force landed in France and marched to the Western Front.

The first significant battle at sea took place on the 28th of August, when a British naval squadron sunk three

German cruisers off the coast of Helgoland. The British had a superior navy, and were able to enforce a blockade in the North Sea. The aim was to prevent supplies from reaching the Central Powers (The remaining members of the Triple Alliance). The blockade lasted from 1914 until 1919, when it was lifted eight months after armistice.

At Mons, on the frontier between Belgium and France, the British Expeditionary Force attempted to hold land against the advancing German forces. Britain inflicted a fair deal of damage to the Germans, but it left was heavily outnumbered and vulnerable following the retreat of France's Fifth Army. Britain too was forced to withdraw.

On the 5th of September, British and French forces halted their retreat and held ground at the Marne River to prevent the German incursion from reaching Paris. The following day, the Germans caught up with the Allied forces and the Battle of the Marne began. The Allied efforts succeeded in preventing the advancing German force from reaching Paris, and pushed them back towards the border--but at the combined cost of over half a million men from each side.

In the weeks that followed, Allied and Central Powers began a "Race to the Sea", an attempt by both sides to gain ground in unoccupied territory along the French northern flank. There were a total of twelve battles fought during this time, culminating at the Battle of Ypres. From that point, both Allied and Central Powers began a new tactic by which to hold and gain ground: trench-warfare.

Both sides dug trenches that stretched from the Channel to Switzerland. The vast trench networks, which ran approximately three hundred fifty and miles, formed the Western Front.

In August, Britain, France and Germany began a series of assaults in Africa. From August 9th to the 26th, Britain and France mounted a successful offensive into German-occupied Togoland, forcing the German army to surrender or desert. Meanwhile, on the 15th, German forces advanced into British-controlled Kenya and seized the town of Taveta.

On the 17th of August, Russia invaded East Prussia. The intention was to gain land from the German forces whilst keeping them occupied on the Eastern Front, thereby relieving some pressure on the Allied forces on the Western Front. However, Germany scored a huge victory at the end of August in the Battle of Tannenberg. Germany crushed Russia's Second Army. Between the 7th and 14th of September, the Russian armies were purged from Prussia by German forces and pushed back behind the Eastern Front. Towards the end of August, and into early September, Austria-Hungary failed to make any significant gains against Serbia and was forced to retreat from its botched invasion into Russia.

The world was now at war. Japan had stayed true to its agreement with its British allies and declared war on Germany. The Ottoman Empire had joined the Central Powers and quickly closed the Dardanelles strait, a vital shipping route, to Allied forces. European colonies in Africa, Asia and the Middle East began maneuvers to weaken the other sides' forces and hold territory.

The war heralded new advancements in technological warfare. The German U-boat (submarines) had proven to be an effective attacker of British warships.

1914 also saw the first use of airplanes in the theatre of war. Chiefly used for reconnaissance at the outbreak of the war, the airplane was quickly established as a vital and deadly tool in aiding military operations.

Christmas brought a brief truce to The Western Front. Allied and Central forces climbed out of their trenches and played sports, ate and drank together and played music--which provided festive respite from the bitter winter conflict. However, the truce was very short lived, and in the days that followed, enemies who had become friends retook their arms and aimed their sights at one another.

The Great War marched into the New Year, having vastly overrun its predicted length. Thousands had been lost, towns had been destroyed and people displaced. The numbers far outweighed the pre-war estimations. A heavy cloud had descended on Europe, shrouding it in the shadow of war.

Chapter Two

1915 - The Dawn Of The Industrialized War

The global conflict was producing new methods of warfare. A lack of anything more than meager and narrow victories by all sides, acquired by outdated tactics, necessitated newer strategies and equipment. On the Western Front, trench-warfare was the main method by which Allied and Central forces attempted to capture and defend land. Germany quickly saw the potential of rapid firing machine guns and employed them throughout their trenches. Allied forces were slower in adopting the weapon, but after witnessing the devastation it had caused to their own forces, they began adding the machine gun to their arsenal.

Germany utilized the power of the U-boat and installed a blockade in around the British Isles to stop supply vessels from reaching British ports. This obstacle to vital cargo was a direct and efficient counter response to the North Sea blockade.

The first ever bombing raid in Britain occurred on the 19th of January, carried out by two German zeppelins-- giant airships filled with hydrogen. The zeppelins dropped a number of bombs on Great Yarmouth, Sheringham and Kings Lynn, which resulted in four civilian deaths and heavy destruction to buildings.

On the 23rd of January, Britain intercepted German transmissions detailing plans of a naval sortie near Dodder Bank in the North Sea. The British Navy was ordered to intercept and repel the German squadron. The Battle of Dodder Bank commenced on the 24th, which resulted in the loss of a German battleship and damage to the squadron. The British fleet was successful in repelling the German squadron, but not in sinking it.

On the 28th, German and Ottoman forces began an assault on the British held Suez Canal in an attempt to gain control of another significant shipping route. But by February 3rd, the British had quashed the assault. The German and Ottoman forces sustained a large number of casualties.

On the Eastern Front, German forces began using chemical weapons--a new device of death designed to bring a more resolute and quick ending to battles.

The Germans unleashed xylyl bromide on the Russian forces at the Battle of Bolimów, but the attack backfired when the wind blew the chemical back over German lines. Luckily for the German forces, a combination of cold weather and the primitive concentration of the deadly mist prevented the xylyl bromide from doing too much harm. In reaction to the failed chemical assault, the Germans called off the attack.

The Battle of Bolimów preluded the more successful German assault that was launched on February the 7th, which became known as The Second Battle of the Masurian Lake. Field Marshal von Hindenburg led the Central forces in an attack, which wiped out over two hundred thousand Russian soldiers and secured German victory.

February 19th saw the arrival of Allied warships at the Dardanelles, with ambitions to reopen the strait and attack the Turkish capital, Constantinople – modern Istanbul. It was hoped that, in witnessing the true might of the Allied navy, Turkey would be crushed and surrender. It would have been a heavy blow to the Central Powers; with Turkey out of the war, the Allies could reopen the Dardanelles, the vital shipping route that connected Europe to Asia. However, large-scale damage to ships from mines and shore defenses scuppered the Allied efforts; the attack was halted.

Between the 10th and 13th of March, on the Western Front, the three-day Battle of Neuve Chapelle took place, carried out by British and Indian forces, in an attempt to breach German lines. It was hoped that a surge for the Aubers Ridge behind the German Front would compromise the road and rail networks that fed the German lines. Though counted as a tactical victory for the British, German defenses ultimately subdued the surge.

Russia gained a hefty victory, at the expense of Austro-Hungarian forces, during the Siege of Przemyśl on March 22nd, following a hundred and thirty-three-day siege - the longest of the entire war. Casualties were high on both sides, but its leaders lauded the clear Russian victory; Russia had faced a number of heavy defeats up to that point. Meanwhile, the total number of casualties suffered by Austria-Hungary since the war started was over two million.

On April 22nd, during the Second Battle of Ypres, the Germans attacked Allied forces using Chlorine gas, which choked over seven thousand soldiers – three-hundred and fifty of whom died from their injuries. The gas attack took the Allies by surprise; a new weapon had found its place on the battlefield.

By the end of the battle, the town had been devastated by artillery bombardments. Both sides suffered heavy losses, but the majority was firmly on the Allied side, with over eighty thousand lost. There were no clear victors.

The Ottoman Empire began the annexation of up to a million Armenians from its Turkish regions--leading to the Armenian Genocide. The Armenians had suffered long and terrible persecution, and were viewed by the Young Turks of the Ottoman Empire as a people of differing religious and political allegiances. The able-bodied Armenian men were subjected to conscription, hard labor and murder. The women, children and elders were driven into the Syrian Desert without food or water and left to die. The genocide prompted outrage from the Allies who decreed the annexation a crime against humanity.

On April 25th, a huge Allied force consisting of English, French and Indian troops, as well as ANZAC (Australian and New Zealand Army Corps), landed in Gallipoli. The objective was to take out the heavy defenses that lined the Dardanelles so that Allied ships could reach Constantinople and blow it apart. It was believed that the assault would be a quick win for the Allies, but the Turks were prepared and had amassed a virtually impenetrable defense force. When the Allies landed on the Gallipoli peninsula, they were met with extreme force and were pinned on the beach for over twenty-four hours. The water that lapped the beaches ran red with Allied blood. Meanwhile, the Anzac forces landed on the wrong beach, having lost their bearings in the dark, and faced an impossible climb up treacherous cliffs, facing the onslaught of Turkish forces.

The Eastern Front was falling to the Central Powers. On May 1st, the Germans embarked on the Gorlice–Tarnów Offensive, an assault into Russian lines to alleviate the pressure of Russian advancements on Austro-Hungarian forces. It won a spectacular victory for the Central Powers, who were able to push back the Russian armies and regain control of Przemyśl.

On May 7th, German U-boat SM U-20 torpedoed the British ocean liner the RMS Lusitania off the Irish coast. The liner went down with over one thousand one hundred souls, sparing seven hundred and sixty-four. The liner had been carrying American and European passengers from New York to Liverpool. It had also been hauling a heavy load of ammunition and supplies for British forces. The Germans reasoned that such cargo constituted the sinking, but Allied and US governments denounced it as an attack on civilians. The sinking quickly became an iconic moment of the war, signaling a public shift away from American neutrality.

On the Western Front, May 9th, Allied forces began the second battle of Artois against the Central Powers. It was a costly offensive for the Allies, who lost over a hundred and thirty thousand men. The advance failed, with the Allies capturing barely more than a mile of land. The German forces stood strong.

On May 23rd, Italy betrayed its declaration of neutrality and joined the Allies after assurances that it would receive support in acquiring land from Austria-Hungary. She began her first major offensive against Austria-Hungary in the First Battle of Isonzo, along the Italian frontier. Though the Italians outnumbered the Austro-Hungarian forces significantly, the long uphill charge required to reach the enemy lines gave the Central Powers an advantage, and they were able to hold their position. That same day, Germany introduced a new weapon into the fray: the Fokker Eindecker--a monoplane with the first mounted machine gun that synchronized with the aircraft's propeller, giving it the capability to shoot through the propeller without hitting it. This drastically shifted the German's aerial advantage.

Between July and August, the Fokker monoplane had secured air superiority for the Germans above the Western Front. It wasn't until 1916, when Allied air forces introduced aircraft with similar synchronized firepower, that the balance of power was shifted.

In July, The Russians commenced their huge withdrawal from the Galicia-Poland salient on the Eastern Front, allowing Central Powers to make large gains including occupying Warsaw and Ivangorod on August 5th. The "Great Russian Retreat" lasted until September, when Russia took advantage of the ailing, battle worn Austro-German forces and stopped their advance.

The August offensive took place between the 6th through to the 29th. Allies supplied reinforcements to their forces on the Gallipoli peninsula in a final attempt to achieve their objective against the Ottoman Empire. The conflict had been long and costly for both sides. Conditions were terrible and losses were high, but the Allies failed to take any significant ground.

After another passenger liner, the SS Arabic, was torpedoed by a German U-boat - not far from the wreck of the Lusitania - the United States demanded that the German U-boat blockade be lifted for civilian vessels. Germany agreed to loosen its U-boat operations in the Atlantic.

On September 8th, following the Russian retreat from Galicia and Poland, Tsar Nicholas II took control of Russian operations and dismissed Grand Duke Nicholas Nikolayevich as Commander-in-Chief.

Towards the end of September, the Allied forces on the Western Front mounted a huge campaign in order to seize land from Central Powers in France and Belgium. The first was the Third Battle of Artois on the 25th; a French attempt, following heavy artillery bombardment, to push into enemy lines. The French managed some progress in breaching the German first line, and captured the Souchez village--but they failed to penetrate the German's second line and were halted.

In the Battle of Loos, the British launched their largest offensive of the year. They utilized poison gas and tried to push back the German lines, but failed to make significant headway and suffered heavy losses, despite outnumbering the German forces.

The French carried out the final offensive at the Second Battle of Champagne. Initially they made limited gains and captured a few thousand German troops, but they ran low on ammunition. The Germans then staged a counter-attack and pushed back the French forces. The offensive was called off until more ammunition could be sent to the front. The German forces suffered nearly one hundred and fifty thousand losses; the Allies sustained over two hundred thousand.

In October, Bulgaria allied with the Central Powers and declared war on Serbia. In response, the Allies declared war on Bulgaria and quickly deployed forces in Salonika, Greece – much to the dismay of the Greek Government. The Allies hoped that they could deliver support to Serbia before a main offensive by the Central Powers could begin. However, the Central Powers, with their new Bulgarian allies, invaded Serbia and overtook it in a mere two months.

By the 27th of November, the Serbian army had been overrun. It had retreated to the Adriatic Sea where the few who made it were evacuated by Allied fleets. Serbia suffered the loss of over a third of its entire army.

When winter came, the Central Powers rejoiced over its highly successful year. It had held off major offensives on the Western Front and gained superiority in the air. They had made significant gains on the Eastern Front against Russia and they had defeated Serbia.

Yet it had been a very deadly year for both sides - and there was no end in sight. There had been major technological breakthroughs in the air, on the sea and in the field of battle. U-boats had checkmated the British naval blockade, German aircraft fitted with synchronized machine guns were the scourge of the skies, and poison gas had proven to be more deadly than effective.

Advances in intelligence gave both sides hitherto impossible advantages, and though in its infancy, new methods of reconnaissance and the interception of enemy communications were to totally transform modern warfare forever.

Chapter Three

1916 - Unrelenting Bloodshed

1916 was one of the bloodiest years of the First World War. It was the year that the infamous battles of the Somme and Verdun claimed over two million lives in just a few months. The war had been raging for far longer than either side had anticipated, and involved well over three-quarters of the globe.

By the New Year, The Central Powers held the advantage over the Allied forces, even as both sides had suffered catastrophic losses.

In response to demands from the United States, Germany had loosened its grip over the Atlantic by ordering its U-boats not to attack civilian vessels. Britain maintained its naval blockade in the North Sea, preventing merchant vessels from reaching Germany. Both the Allies and Central Powers were struggling to access supplies from overseas.

On the Western Front, Germany retained air superiority thanks to technological advancements in aviation and armaments. On the ground, young men languished in sodden trenches; many succumbed to gangrene and illness brought on by the atrocious living conditions.

Russian forces had halted their retreat from the Eastern Front, regrouped, and organized a firm stand against the tired and frostbitten Central Powers. Their retreat was over; they had mobilized to secure their lines and engage the oncoming German and Austro-Hungarian forces.

The Allies had suffered a terrible defeat at the hands of the Ottoman Empire on the Gallipoli peninsula. However, Allied forces had succeeded in taking control of the eastern end of the Dardanelles by deploying anti-submarine nets that obstructed German U-boats from reaching Constantinople.

Eight months after the Allied landing, they were forced to evacuate. The Allies and Anzac forces masterminded a brilliant evacuation of the peninsula. Despite the massive advantage the Turks had by holding the higher ground, Allied and Anzac forces were able to slip away right under their noses by using a series of quick skirmish strategies. Retreating forces laid low in trenches for days on end until the Turkish forces came to investigate - falling into an ambush. The Allies and Anzac rigged mechanisms of water containers attached by string to rifle triggers; once full, the container would pull the string and the rifle would effectively "self-shoot". These and a number of sleight of hand tactics enabled the Allies and Anzacs to sneak away, escaping with very few losses. The Allied Governments raged over the painful irony that evacuating was the most successful part of the Gallipoli campaign.

In America, President Woodrow Wilson attempted to arrange peace negotiations between the warring nations of Europe, but the plans failed when no agreement could be reached. America would later enter the war in 1917.

In the first few weeks of January, Austro-Hungarian forces continued to inflict defeat on Serbia and its allies by capturing the Kingdom of Montenegro. Though Serbia's allies were able to hold off the superior Austro-Hungarian army at the Battle of Mojkovac, allowing the remaining defeated Serbian troops to escape to the Albanian mountains, the Montenegrin forces were eventually overcome and Montenegro fell to the invading Austrian army.

On the Russian/Ottoman frontier, the Russians mounted the month long Erzurum Offensive, part of the Caucasus Campaign against Turkish forces. It was a surprise offensive, mounted whilst the Russians retained the advantage of facing a limited Ottoman army in the midst of regrouping their troops after Gallipoli. It was a costly incursion but resulted in the capture of the fortified city of Erzurum, which held tactical significance - it gave the Russians a land advantage and the opportunity to continue pushing forward. The loss of Erzurum quickly ended Turkish enthusiasm over their victory at Gallipoli.

Towards the end of January and into February, Allied forces were able to defeat the Germans in Cameroon after seventeen deadly months of aggression. The victory massively reduced German control in Africa, leaving just one colony in German East Africa on the border of British East Africa and the Belgian Congo. After the fall of Cameroon, Africa was ostensibly under Allied control.

At the end of January, the United Kingdom, owing to a lack of crucial volunteers, legislated conscription for single men aged between eighteen and forty as the war grew longer and more costly.

On February 21st, the Germans began a nine-month long offensive against French forces at the historical French city of Verdun. The attack began with half a day of artillery bombardment, designed to pulverize French defenses and trench networks. With the French defenses in rubble, the German forces made light work of capturing the demolished lines and acquired wide swathes of territory along the Meuse River. However, the German offensive was halted when the French regrouped with additional reinforcements and managed to contain the German advance.

By March, the winter had turned to spring, and the German offensive stalled due to the frozen ground thawing, leaving it impossible to traverse. Some of their equipment became bogged down in the mud and was rendered unusable.

On the 6th, after the ground had hardened, the Germans resumed their attack of Verdun from the west side of the Meuse. They aimed for Côte 304 and Le Mort-Homme, two heavily defended hills that offered strategic advantage over the battlefield. But the French dug in, utilizing the advantage of higher ground to fight off their attackers; only partial areas of the hillsides fell to the German forces. It had been a costly advance with minimal gains.

On the 18th of March, Russian forces launched a fairly rushed offensive against the Central Powers at Lake Naroch on the Eastern Front. The offensive was at the request of Marshal Joseph Joffre, commander-in-chief of the French side, who hoped that it would divert sections of the German forces to the Eastern Front, limiting their capabilities at Verdun. However, due to the hasty organization of the rushed offensive and poor reconnaissance that led to a relatively ineffectual artillery barrage, the attack was a complete disaster. Russian forces lost five times as many men as the Central Powers.

In the final days of April, republicans in Ireland launched an insurrection against the British forces in protest of British rule. The six-day revolt became known as the Easter Rising, a rebellion which saw thousands of Irish revolutionaries fight to gain an independent Ireland--free of monarchical and British governmental rule.

The British promptly extinguished the uprising, which led to the unconditional surrender of the republicans on the 29th of April. Over five hundred were killed and over three thousand arrested, many of who played no part in the uprising.

After the surrender, many of the leaders of the revolt were executed for their role in the uprising. Ireland remained under martial law until 1920 when the Restoration of Order in Ireland Act came into effect.

On April 29th, following a long and exhausting five-month siege at Kut-al-Amara in Mesopotamia - modern-day Iraq - British and Indian soldiers surrendered en-masse to Turkish forces after four failed attempts to recapture the once Allied-occupied town from the Ottomans. The surrender was one of the largest in British history. Thirteen thousand soldiers were led to a prison camp in Aleppo; most these soldiers died whilst imprisoned. It was a humiliating loss for the British.

On May 3rd, German forces at Verdun launched their second attack on the west bank of the river Meuse. After three hard days of combat, they succeeded in capturing the Côte 304 and Le Mort-Homme hills from the French. The successful attack gained them the advantage of higher ground from where they could launch further attacks whilst being able to hold their position.

Towards the end of May, The British Royal Navy's Grand Fleet engaged the German Navy's High Seas Fleet in the North Sea in what became known as the Battle of Jutland.

In an effort to dismantle the British blockade, the Germans planned to lure part of the British Fleet into engagement with their heavier ships. The Germans knew that their navy was inferior to their British counterparts, so they couldn't mount a full attack without running the risk of being out-gunned. At this point, Germany was feeling the effects of the British blockade. She knew that she had to cripple part of the British North Sea fleet in order to compromise the blockade and allow merchant ships to deliver vital supplies.

On May 3rd, after intercepting German communications about a mounting sea offensive, an initial squadron of British battle cruisers sailed away from the main fleet to scout for the German High Seas Fleet. By late afternoon, the British battle cruisers met with German cruisers not far from where the High Seas fleet was positioned. After a brief exchange of fire, the British ships turned around and headed back to the main fleet. The High Seas fleet followed.

As the sun set that evening, the two fleets met and opened fire. Late in the evening, after many hours of fighting and many lives lost, the German fleet was able to break through a rear vanguard of the British fleet that had boxed them in, and managed to escape to the fleet's main port. By the end of the great sea battle, the British had lost fourteen of its 151-strong fleet; the Germans had lost eleven of their ninety-nine. Though neither side was really victorious, both claimed to have won the battle. The German Navy returned to port and remained there until the end of the war. The British Navy resumed the North Sea blockade.

By the summer, the Central Powers in Europe were starting to feel the squeeze of the advancing Russian army as it made strong gains against Austro-Hungarian forces along the Rumanian frontier. The Italians were slowly but surely creeping into the southern regions of Austria-Hungary, and the Allies on the Western Front held their position against German advances. The Central Powers had to reshuffle its forces in order to shore up the Austro-Hungarian border on the Eastern Front against the slowly advancing Russians.

On June 24th, a seven-day Allied artillery bombardment of German trenches began near the river Somme. The hope was that such a heavy strike would cripple German defenses, paving the way for the much larger offensive that was to follow. Over a million shells fell over a fifteen mile stretch of German lines, but it failed to inflict the level of damage needed to allow the quick victory the Allies had hoped for.

The first stage of the brutal Battle of the Somme commenced on July 1st. Initially, the Allied forces made some significant gains against the compromised German defenses. However, as the bloody day moved on, the Germans dealt the British a tremendous defeat.

On the first day of the Battle of the Somme, British forces lost over nineteen thousand troops; over thirty-eight thousand more were injured. It remains one of the bloodiest days in modern military history.

The battle raged on as each side desperately clung to just yards of land. At Verdun, German forces had again engaged with the French whilst the battle at the Somme continued simultaneously; by the end of August, the Germans had called off the attack and began to focus their forces at the Somme, as Verdun had been valiantly defended by her children. Both sides sustained casualties of over three hundred thousand each.

On September 15th, a new weapon joined the fight - a weapon that was to secure itself as one of the most powerful and iconic tools of modern warfare: the tank.

The British Mark 1 tank grumbled onto the battlefield and engaged the German forces. Yet the primitive beast was limited; it suffered endless mechanical problems and didn't function as efficiently as the British had hoped, and it certainly didn't secure the Allies victory on the Somme.

The Allies finally put an end to the deadly Somme offensive on the 18th of November. They had managed to gain around five miles from the Germans, pushing them further back behind their lines, but the advance certainly fell short of the type of gains the Allied generals had hoped they'd acquire. The death toll was staggering; well over a million Allied and German soldiers had been massacred in the deadly marshland that separated the trenches. The Somme quickly became a testament to the horrors of war and the desperate need for newer tactics. The massive loss suffered for barely any ground gained was unjustifiable in public opinion.

By the end of 1916, the death toll had risen by millions, chiefly due to the Battle of the Somme and Verdun, though it had been a year of unfathomable losses for both sides. More countries had declared war on the Central Powers. Italy, Portugal and Romania had joined the Allies. The Arab revolt, spearheaded by T.E Lawrence (Lawrence of Arabia), had begun cutting into the Ottoman lines and had made headway. Most Allied countries had also declared war on Bulgaria, and the world was awaiting word from the United States.

The US had issued severe threats that it would cut diplomatic ties with Germany if she failed to suppress her U-boat operations. Three ships carrying US citizens had been sunk by U-boats. The hope of successful peace talks had all but failed; US involvement began to seem likelier by the day.

Chapter Four

1917 - Revolution, Revelation and Catastrophe

By 1917, both sides appeared less committed to gaining the tactical advantage than they were to the mass slaughter of the other sides' forces. The Central Powers were hemmed in between three fronts. They'd lost a great deal of power in Africa, the Western Front was in a perpetual stalemate and the Russians had stalled their advance on the Eastern Front. Fearing US involvement after she resumed her U-boat operations, Germany was feeling the pressure. Britain was Germany's strongest obstacle; she knew that she had to strangle Britain into surrender to stand any chance of securing victory of The Great War.

In mid-January, British intelligence intercepted a communication from the German Foreign Office. The communication was decoded and revealed a telegram sent by the State Secretary for Foreign Affairs, Alfred Zimmermann, to the German embassy in Mexico. This infamous missive became known as the "Zimmerman Telegram", revealing a proposition of alliance between Germany and Mexico; Germany would provide the necessary support for an attack on the southern states to reclaim historic land taken from Mexico by the United States. The telegram was quickly dispatched to the US government. The plan was announced to the US public and demand for US intervention increased pressure on Washington to re-evaluate its position of neutrality.

On February 1st, Germany resumed its U-boat blockade with the intention of crippling Britain by preventing food and resources from reaching its shores. German U-boats began indiscriminate attacks on merchant ships, including the US steamer S.S Housatonic. On February 3rd, the US finally ended diplomatic ties with Germany in response to the attack. Germany was playing a dangerous game, but it knew that in order to triumph over the Allied forces, Britain had to be heavily compromised.

In Mesopotamia, the British had regrouped after the fall of Kut al-Amara and the surrender of British troops to the Turks. It was yet another humiliating defeat for the British Army. In response, London prioritized a second siege to reclaim the city from the Ottomans.

On the 23rd, the fresh surge of British troops reclaimed the city in The Second Battle of Kut. The British drove out the Turkish forces while sustaining three times fewer casualties than their adversaries. On March 8th, the victorious British forces marched on to claim Baghdad within three days.

In Russia, mass demonstrations by civilians in St Petersburg, fuelled by anger over the incredible losses Russia had sustained on the Eastern Front, developed into a violent revolution against Tsar Nicholas II. In the days that followed, a mutiny by Russian forces strengthened the revolution; Tsar Nicholas II was forced to abdicate on March 15th and appoint a provisional government to run the war efforts. The new leadership was quickly established, and the Allies urged the new Russian government to maintain the Eastern Front against the Central Powers.

On the 26th of March, British forces advanced into southern Palestine from Egypt. Their goal was to capture the city of Gaza from Ottoman control. The British did well; they scored land and nearly captured the city. However, they withdrew from Gaza over concerns that the dark of night would be detrimental to the occupation, and the Ottoman reinforcements were much larger than had been anticipated. This withdrawal led to British defeat.

In April, the Second Battle for Gaza began. The British were eager to try and recapture the town following the failure of their first attempt, but this time they were met with strengthened defenses and the deadly Ottoman infantry. The British were killed in the hundreds; the Ottomans held the town.

On April 2nd, Woodrow Wilson, the President of the United States, gathered the US Congress to seek approval for a declaration of war against Germany. After their deliberation, Wilson was provided the authority he needed on April 6th, and the United States declared war on Germany.

April proved to be a highly successful month for the German navy and air force. German U-boats surpassed their targets for sinking merchant vessels destined for Britain. In the skies over the Western Front, German aircraft downed British fighters at a vastly superior rate, shooting down over one hundred and fifty aircraft in

April alone. During this period, which became known as Bloody April, British pilots had a life expectancy of just two to three weeks. Despite this, the Royal Flying Corps was refused the use of parachutes; it was reasoned that pilots would be more likely to bail out and let their aircraft fall into the hands of the Germans if they had parachutes.

On April 9th, the Allied forces launched the Second Battle of Arras on the Western Front. British, Canadian, and Anzac forces attacked the German defenses. The battle was part of a larger offensive coinciding with a French offensive further south that was hoped would ultimately break through the German lines and lead to a war of movement that would repulse the German forces. It was hoped that if the offensives were successful, they would end the war in forty days.

On the first day of the offensive, the British made headway into the German lines, capturing over three miles of territory. The Canadians captured the strategically important higher ground at Vimy Ridge, but at a high cost. Further south, the Allied forces failed to secure any real ground, as they were hounded by major German defenses.

By the end of the first day, strong groundwork in the north had secured the Allies some strategic gains, albeit with heavy losses. However, as the battle progressed the Allies failed to utilize their advantage, as was the case in the first Battle of Arras, and the Germans managed to shore up their new lines. It was a costly Allied victory that eventually stalled; stalemate returned to the Western Front once more.

On April 16th, The French began their part of the assault along a twenty-five-mile stretch of the German Lines just south of the "Hindenburg Line"--a heavy line of German defenses. It was known as the "Nivelle Offensive", as it was masterminded by France's new Commander-in-Chief, Robert Nivelle.

The attack was designed to be the most crucial element of the entire Allied April offensive. The plan was to smash through the German lines whilst the British were occupying German forces further north at Arras. Once through, the French were to loop around and meet with the British to the north and chase the Germans back until they surrendered.

The first stage of the attack secured the French a partial capture of German lines. The French advanced using the "Barrage Tactic", which involved waves of men advancing behind and in front of strong Artillery shelling. However, the advance didn't progress as quickly as expected; the Germans obtained good intelligence from aerial reconnaissance photographs and quickly grasped the French plans. The offensive failed miserably and incurred major losses in exchange for insignificant gains. General Nivelle was promptly dismissed from his position.

The failure of the Nivelle Offensive, along with the terrible living conditions in the trenches, caused about half of the French divisions to refuse orders and mutiny. Nivelle's successor General Henri Petain, "The Hero of

Verdun", ordered suppression of the resistance by carrying out large numbers of arrests and executions to set an example. He was then quickly dispatched to the Western Front to restore order. There he promised not to command another assault that would incur masses of casualties in the aim of securing minor gains. Soldiers were sick of the ongoing war of attrition.

For more than a year, British, Australian and Canadian soldiers had been digging a tunnel and laying mines under the Messines Ridge, a position held by the Germans. On June 7th, the British detonated the nineteen mines, which triggering a massive explosion that wiped out over ten thousand German soldiers in an instant. The Allies then moved in and forced the Germans to fall back to a position further east of the battered Ridge.

On June 13th, a squadron of twenty-two Gotha G.IV bombers carried out the first bombing raid on London using airplanes (previous bombing raids over England had been carried out by zeppelins). The bombs killed over a hundred and fifty people and wounded a further four hundred.

On July the 1st, the first batch of American troops landed at the Western Front. On the 2nd, King Constantine of Greece abdicated, giving way to a pro-Allied democratic government that swiftly joined the Allies.

Also on July 1st, the Russians mounted their final, and unsuccessful, offensive against the Central Powers on the Eastern Front. The Kerensky Offensive began at Galicia with the intention of fighting all the way to the city of Lviv. The Russians bombarded the Central Powers with massive shelling and were initially able to make some gains into enemy lines, but the Central Powers stood firm and were able to contain the Russian advance.

In the Russian ranks, mutiny was thick in the air. Divisions of men refused to follow their officers into battle, leaving combat to the cavalry and artillery, which was limited without their infantry backup. The clumsy assault, paired with disobedience, caused the Russian army to fall apart. The Central Powers seized the advantage and smashed the Russian forces with a deadly counter-attack. The remaining Russian soldiers fled back to their lines.

On the 6th of June, an Arab assault, co-led by T.E. Lawrence, seized the Jordanian port of Aqaba. The port allowed access to regional Allies in order to assist the British in their fight against the Ottoman Empire.

On July 13th, British forces, then the prime defenders on the Western Front, began their third offensive at Ypres. It was yet another attempt to break through the German lines. It became known as the Battle of Passchendaele. The British managed to capture a section of the German front line, but were prevented from proceeding due to readied artillery and atrocious weather conditions that turned No Man's Land into a swamp.

In August, the battle resumed. The British's main aim was to take out the German artillery that had held them up, but the attack failed and once again the Allies made little to no ground. The failure halted the campaign, whilst the Allied higher-ups reviewed their strategy.

On the Eastern Front, the Germans secured their final victory over the Russians in the Battle of Jugla. The Germans, who had employed new methods of attack, saw out the Russian forces from the town of Riga. It effectively led to the collapse of the Eastern Front.

In late October, Austro-Hungarian and German forces engaged the Italian army in the Battle of Caporetto on the Italian frontier. The Central Powers succeeded in weakening the Italian army and managed to push them back over sixty miles to the south where, exhausted and battered, over three hundred thousand Italian soldiers surrendered to the Central Powers and more than four hundred thousand fled. British and French forces scrambled to redeploy divisions from the Western Front to aid the Italians, but the advance of the Central Powers was too extreme.

On November 6th, Canadian troops succeeded in capturing the village of Passchendaele, but it was a limited victory. After three months of sodden, deadly warfare, the Allied offensive was cancelled. Both sides sustained over two hundred thousand casualties all for piecemeal territory gains.

On November 7th to the 8th, the Bolshevik party in Russia, led by Vladimir Lenin and Leon Trotsky, staged the October Revolution, which dissolved the Russian provisional government and supplanted it with a Marxist-Soviet government. The revolution put an end to Russian involvement in the Great War, and shortly after the takeover, Russia signed an armistice agreement with Germany.

With the Eastern Front gone, the Allies and Central Powers knew that victory for either side was dependent upon American reinforcements. In late November, the British staged an attack at Cambrai, an important rail supply point for the German forces. The Battle of Cambrai was the first time heavy tank divisions were deployed on the battlefield. Nearly four hundred metal clad machines pushed into German lines and enabled the British forces to advance and capture over five miles of land. However, as was much of the story of British successes in The Great War, the gains weren't exploited and the Germans returned with heavy reinforcements. After their five-mile trek, the tanks began to falter and posed little threat to the German counter attack.

Winter arrived and froze No Man's Land. Russia had begun the year ruled by the last figure of a three-hundred-year-old dynasty, but by the end of the year it was a Communist/Bolshevik nation. The Germans no longer had to fight on the Eastern Front and instead were freed to focus their efforts on the Austro-Hungarian frontier and the Western Front.

But where one giant fell, another awoke. All eyes were on the Americans. The Central Powers knew that if it didn't act fast, the Americans could very easily turn the tide in favor of the Allies. The world watched as the Great War entered its final year.

Chapter Five

1918 - The Great War At An End

The war that had been sparked by the assassination of a Hungarian official had spread to every corner of the world, and had been raging for over three and a half years. The death toll of soldiers and civilians across Europe had risen into the millions. Once-flourishing towns had been flattened and laid to waste, which routed their populations and changed the landscape of Europe forever.

The Eastern Front had fallen due to the revolution in Russia, and its transformation into a Communist nation allowed Germany to focus primarily on the Western Front. The addition of American troops that arrived daily on the Allied lines, and the North Sea blockade that prevented sorely needed supplies from reaching Germany, increased German desperation to claim something from a war that was likely going to end in defeat. Germany feared that unless she made rapid gains, the Americans would flood the Allied lines and make German victory impossible.

On January 8th, President Wilson detailed his fourteen-point peace plan. One of the defining motions of the plan was to form a "General Association of Nations" (which became the United Nations) to ensure that a global conflict of such magnitude wouldn't be repeated. But the context of the plan failed to inspire the governments of the warring nations of Europe. The war had been long and costly. It had been a vicious war of attrition, ergo forgiveness and association seemed like a fairy-tale forged from unwitting American idealism.

On the 3rd of March, the Soviet Russian Bolsheviks signed the Treaty of Brest-Litovsk with Germany, which finalized their armistice agreement. The treaty demanded that over a quarter of official Russian territory be handed over to the Central Powers. Part of the territory was to be allocated to the Ukrainian People's Republic in a promise of protection of their sovereignty. The Soviets also had to give away a great deal of their industries and rail networks to Germany.

The treaty officially ended the war on the Eastern Front, which enabled Germany to remove over half a million troops and deploy them along the Western Front to strengthen their stance against the Allies. This redeployment allowed Germany to plan what it hoped would be its final push of The Great War, an advance to capture key areas of France and obliterate the stretched Allied forces before the Americans could tip the advantage.

On March 21st, the Germans began the first phase of their massive spring offensive, masterminded by General Ludendorff. With the arrival of new troops from the Eastern Front trained in new storm trooper tactics, which gave the Germans the edge on speed, infiltration and annihilation, the Germans held a strong presence on the battlefield; they easily outnumbered the Allied forces.

Operation Michael began with a five-hour long artillery bombardment, then a huge German push from the Hindenburg Line into Allied territory. The aim was to break the British lines and capture vital Channel ports, repelling the Allies on the way.

The first stage won the Germans large gains along the front as they pushed the beleaguered British troops towards the sea. The Germans managed to reclaim territory they'd lost in the Battle of the Somme; Ludendorff then focused German efforts on splitting apart the French and British troops and driving both into the sea.

When the initial successes of the offensive made clear to the Allies that it would likely end in German victory, the British and French agreed to appoint a Supreme Commander to preside over the Western Front and unify Allied strategy. Ferdinand Foch was selected to replace the various commanders along the front in order to lead the Allied defense and counter-attacks.

The second stage of Ludendorff's offensive began on April 9th. Operation Georgette was designed to recapture the city of Ypres from the British and continue to push the British forces back to the coast, cutting them off from the French and suppressing both sides. The Germans were able to push the British out of Ypres, recapture the Passchendaele Ridge and repulse the British over three miles to the northeast. The gains were good, but German momentum couldn't be maintained and their advance was thwarted by Allied reinforcements who eventually held their position and seriously hindered the German advance, massacring them in the process.

April saw a significant shift in air superiority. Britain was producing some of the best aircraft, and its pilots (known as Aces) were downing German aircraft faster than the Germans could destroy British planes. Additionally, merchant convoys were now sailing with naval escorts, which impacted U-boat attempts to block supplies from reaching Britain. As a result the Allies were able to manufacture aircraft quicker than the deprived German air force.

On the first of April, the Royal Flying Corps and Royal Naval Air Service were combined to form the Royal Air Force. Towards the end of the month, German pilot Manfred von Richthofen - the feared "Red Baron" - was shot down and killed by a British scout aircraft. Von Richthofen was the most prolific Ace of the war, with eighty kills to his name.

On the 27th of May, the Germans began the third stage of their offensive. The objective of the Blücher-Yorck offensive was to address the French troops south of the previous assaults, to continue to separate them from the Allies further north, and capture the Chemin des Dames ridge before the Americans could arrive and exploit the ridge's strategic advantage.

The Germans were highly successful. They drove the Allied forces thirty miles behind the front, taking many prisoners and capturing important defense structures. But as the repulsion neared Paris, the Germans were hindered by a lack of resources and their troops had been pushed to exhaustion. They were halted at the River Marne by American and Allied forces.

By the end of May, a fresh and relatively inexperienced American division captured the village of Cantigny from the Germans, which instilled Allied confidence in American forces. At that point in the war, over seven hundred thousand American troops had arrived in France, with a daily arrival of over ten thousand US troops to support the Allies.

On June 6th, the second division of American troops engaged German forces at the Battle of Belleau Wood. The battle lasted three weeks and resulted in American-Allied victory, but at the loss of over five thousand American troops. It was their first big loss of the war.

On June 9th, the Germans attempted another advance towards Paris in the fourth stage of their Spring Offensive. However, the assault was rushed through planning and was met with a heavy counter-attack from American and Allied troops. The Spring Offensive provided some early success for the Germans, but by the summer it was starting to wane as over a million American troops had arrived in France to support the Allies.

In mid-June, the Austro-Hungarian army began an attack on Italian forces at the Piave River in Italy. The attack was requested by the Germans to help with their offensive on the Western Front; they hoped that the Allies would remove divisions from the Western Front and deploy them on the Italian frontier to support the Italian forces. However, the Italians had learned that an attack was approaching, so they mobilized their artillery to face the Austrian front line. The shelling did some damage and delayed the attack for a while, but it didn't prevent the Austrian advance.

The attack scored the Austrians a brief twelve-mile advantage, but due to a lack of proper provisions and a reluctant army, the Austrians were forced back by the Italians in a counter-attack. By the end of the Battle of the Piave River, the Austrians suffered over one hundred and fifty casualties and, in the face of defeat, many fled over the border. The Italians, who chased off what was left of the Austrian forces, recaptured all the ground that they had lost.

On July 15th, the Germans began their final offensive of the First World War. The Marne-Reims Offensive consisted of two strategic attacks by the Germans against Allied forces, but the Allies were ready for the attack and crushed each German advance, rendering Ludendorff's offensive a failure. The Allies mounted a massive counter-offensive in a final attempt to win the war.

As the summer turned to autumn, Allied forces pushed through the Hindenburg Line and started to make heavy gains against the weakening German forces. The break in the Hindenburg Line marked the beginning of a long German retreat in what became known as the "Hundred Day Offensive".

Between September and October, the collapse of the Central Powers rippled through Europe and the Middle East. On September 29th, the Allies agreed to a Bulgarian armistice after Allied forces in the Baltic regions defeated her. She was the first country of the Central Powers to cease involvement in the war. On the Italian front, at the Battle of Vittorio Veneto, the Austrian army was totally defeated by the Italian forces. Over three hundred thousand tired Austrian troops were taken captive. On October the 30th, the Ottoman Empire signed an armistice agreement with the Allies following the capture of Damascus and Aleppo by Allied forces.

As winter arrived on the Western Front, the German army had been repulsed back to the Belgian and German border. Her soldiers were tired and were suffering from hunger and illness. In the weeks that followed, thousands of German troops surrendered to the Allies.

In the final weeks of the Great War, Germany contacted Washington DC and requested an armistice. Washington agreed, under the proviso that Germany removed her forces from occupied countries and took full responsibility for the war.

At the eleventh hour of the eleventh day of the eleventh month, the guns fell silent on the Western Front. Armistice had been declared; the brutal war was finally over.

Conclusion

The Great War ended with a casualty tally of over thirty-eight million and no real winners. The Central Powers had gained vast amounts of pre-war Russian territory, but their losses were catastrophic. By the autumn of 1918, the Austro-Hungarian Empire dissolved after a number of revolutions ousted the monarchy.

The war had rallied the Russian people against the ruling dynasty and replaced it with a Marxist-Soviet government under the command of Lenin––it was the beginning of the spread of socialism across the world.

The British had divided the Middle East into an array of nations in an attempt to hold onto their wilting imperial ambitions. After the Ottomans signed their armistice agreement with the Allied powers, her empire began to dissolve as Mesopotamia fell under the rule of European powers. The remnants of the empire were purged, and Mesopotamia was divided by new boundaries. Indigenous peoples were removed from their homes and condensed into new areas.

Germany had to accept the entire responsibility for the war and submit to the vast number of crippling sanctions outlined in the Treaty of Versailles, signed at the Paris Peace Conference in 1919. Germany was ordered to relieve a wealth of territory and reduce its borders. In place of Germanic rule, once occupied and suppressed nations were renewed and independent autonomy spread across the region.

The European map was changed--gone were the infallible empires that were laid like thick blankets across the continent. The epoch of the empire was drawing to a close.

Alongside her losses in Europe, Germany's overseas colonies were seized and taken over by European powers, which left the country with a very restricted border and no overseas territories. She was also ordered to massively reduce her armed forces and was instructed not to go beyond the sanctioned targets for personnel and equipment. These sanctions contributed to a great German depression in the decades that followed, and were a prelude to the foreboding conflict that was to descend the world into chaos once again.

Historians remember the First World War as the first real industrialized war. In just four years, both sides had developed new mass-produced weapons that would ultimately go on to play significant roles in modern day conflicts. The airplane proved that not only could it undertake crucial reconnaissance missions, but it was also a speedy and efficient killer. The machine gun became a mainstay of military engagement. The tank showed that it was in its element when smashing through defense lines. These machines of war had been mass produced at home and dispatched quickly to the front line. Production line warfare had begun.

World War One stands among the worst wars to befall humanity, yet the moral remains unclear. So many lives were lost in the desperate rush for tiny stretches of scorched earth. Wave upon wave of men were gunned down and lost to the stolid mud that covered no-mans land. The heavy losses convinced the generals to change their tactics of warfare.

To this day, contention persists as to whether the war could have been avoided. The delicate balance of power hung over Europe like the sword of Damocles; it's difficult to imagine that the weak equilibrium could have been maintained for long.

The world had been wounded and each country involved mourned the loss of her children. Millions had been displaced by the war. It had ended badly, and post-war operations were conducted arrogantly and with limited attention. The balance in Europe began to tip once again; things hadn't been settled and there were debts still to pay. A new conflict was about to echo the first, and what had been learned was to be utilized once more in another horrendous war.

Made in the USA
Columbia, SC
24 November 2018